Wayana

& Master Index

12

Indigenous Peoples of the World
Wayana
& Master Index

Grolier Educational Corporation

SHERMAN TURNPIKE, DANBURY, CONNECTICUT 06816

Published by Grolier Educational Corporation 1995
Danbury, Connecticut

Set ISBN: 0-7172-7470-5
Volume ISBN: *Wayana* 0-7172-7474-8
Library of Congress Number 94-073301

Manufactured in the United States of America.

Contributors

Jennifer Croft *(Ladakhi)* holds a degree in anthropology from Columbia University and is an editor and free-lance writer.

Anne Johnson *(Inuit, Karenni, Mentawai, Naga)* holds a degree from the University of Wisconsin, Madison. She has done extensive research on myths and folk epics from around the world.

Barbara Miller *(Tuareg)* is a Ph.D. candidate in anthropology at New York University. She specializes in ethnographic filmmaking. She has conducted applied urban research and has been involved with developing curricula for museums and schools.

Eugene Murphy, Ph.D. *(Maya)* is an instructor of anthropology at Columbia University. He has produced an ethnographic documentary on Mayan migration and has written extensively on the peoples of Mexico and China.

Roger Rosen *(Endangered Peoples)* is an editor and publisher. He has published material on the indigenous peoples of the former Soviet Union and has edited numerous articles and papers on the plight of indigenous peoples.

Steven Rubenstein, Ph.D. *(Huaorani)* has been awarded grants from the Guggenheim, Fulbright, and MacArthur Foundations and has conducted fieldwork in Brazil, Ecuador, and the United States.

Colleen She *(Miao)* received a master's degree in East Asian studies from Columbia University. She is a free-lance writer and translator.

Jeanne Strazzabosco *(Wayana)* is an instructor in French and Spanish and a free-lance translator and writer whose work regularly addresses the plight of indigenous peoples.

Pegi Vail *(Omo Peoples)* is a Ph.D. candidate in anthropology at New York University. She specializes in visual anthropology and has worked extensively with children's educational programs at museums and schools.

Contents

A large, feathered headdress called an *olok* is essential to the Maraké ceremony. Crowds cheer the first time that the *olok* is displayed.

CHAPTER 1

THE GREAT MARAKÉ

IT IS THE EVE OF THE GREAT MARAKÉ, WHICH IS THE MOST significant ceremony of the Wayana of South America. Every member of the community is busy preparing. Youngsters play games of hunting and fishing and mime while the adults practice rituals that have been performed by their ancestors for hundreds of years.

The Maraké is not a single ritual but an ensemble of several extremely complex ceremonies. For 15 days and nights the Wayana gather in the village. Each day is full of dancing, games, and practice. The atmosphere becomes more and more frenzied as the great day approaches.

Laniki, a ten-year-old Wayana boy, is especially excited this year because it is the first time that he will be allowed to participate in the great tests. As long as he can remember, his family has come to the village of Elae to take part in the Maraké festival. He has watched his entire family participate in the beautiful rituals every year, and now it is his turn.

The godfathers are in the forest collecting the stinging insects for the morning's tests. The godfathers collect wasp nests and stinging ants. Later they will imprison the insects between wicker frames called *kunana*.

Laniki tries not to think about the *kunana*. He hopes to withstand the tests without crying. It is important to endure them without complaint. Those who succeed are praised by the entire village. If Laniki succeeds he will be able to meet the challenges and difficulties of the new year with courage and strength. But for now, he dreams about the evening's festivities, filled with dance and music.

The village women have put the final touches on the ceremonial garments. They have been sewing the intricate clothes for months. Laniki can hardly wait to wear the feathered headdress. He remembers how wonderful his brother looked last year in his *olok*. The 6-foot-high feather headdress made him look like a giant multicolored bird. He still can hear the soft rattle of the leg ornaments worn by his brother and the other participants. He closes his eyes to imagine how he will look in his *olok* and pearls.

Laniki enters the ceremonial hut. Here he is to be dressed. The women begin to drape him in a tunic made of strands of pearls. Laniki stands next to his older brother, Malavete, and admires his garment. He is so proud to be beside his brother that he barely feels the heaviness of the tunic. The pearls alone weigh between 20 and 30 pounds.

Next a many-colored, beautifully woven loincloth is placed on Laniki. He is then given an armadillo flute and a ritual bow and arrow.

Stinging insects are placed between wicker frames and laid against the bodies of Maraké participants.

Laniki knows that the best part is about to come. He and the other participants wait while the godfathers display the *oloks* to the entire population.

Laniki can see that a crowd has formed outside the ceremonial hut. When the godfathers present the *oloks*, the crowd cheers. As the participants are led out, the cheers and cries of the people rise up again. Laniki looks for his mother in the crowd. She went through the test of the Maraké last year to show her support of her husband. This year she helped the other village women prepare the garments. Finally Laniki catches a glimpse of her, and she smiles proudly at her two sons.

At the heart of the Wayana village is the *toukousipan,* where ceremonies are held.

Godfathers have been selected for Laniki and the other participants. Laniki's godfather will encourage and guide him through all the rituals and tests. He places the *olok* upon Laniki's head as the boy's heart beats faster and faster. The time is approaching for the Moloko to appear. The Moloko is the great shaman, the healer and priest of the people.

The shaman appears in the center of the village. Laniki is barely able to contain his excitement. It seems almost as if the Moloko is part of the forest, for his entire body is covered with lianas and leaves. He stands upon a board called an *epa,* which is lying across a small dug-out trench. As the great shaman stamps his feet, a rich powerful sound reverberates through the forest.

As dusk falls, a dance that will last long into the night begins, and the Maraké candidates loudly stamp on the *epa* in an irregular beat. While dancing, they play armadillo flutes, on which they must continuously and untiringly produce the same note. The godfathers are close by and encourage them by fanning them with broad wicker fans. The candidates yell, sing, and imitate animal cries.

Dawn arrives, and Laniki is in the first group to undergo the test of the Maraké at the hands of his godfather. The godfathers come with the *kunana,* wicker frames that contain the stinging insects. Laniki must show his courage and resist pain without a single complaint or sound. He uses all his powers of concentration as his godfather lays the insect-filled frame upon his chest. The insects crawl upon him. He feels the warm sensation of the stings but says nothing and hardly moves.

The next groups to undergo the test are the adolescents and finally the adults. Laniki watches closely. He cannot believe that some of the participants ask to undergo the test a second time with another *kunana.*

The tests are not over yet, however. The participants are taken into the great ceremonial house, the *toukousipan,* to undergo the test of temptation. They receive only water to drink and thin manioc bread to eat for a long period of time. While fasting, they are constantly offered the most succulent of Wayana dishes. Once they have successfully resisted the temptation to eat, their bodies are painted with a reddish stain, and they are led outdoors.

The final rituals are Laniki's favorites. He has been practicing for them all year. He and the other candidates must demonstrate their abilities with the bow and arrow. If only he can hit the target! His father would be so proud of him.

By the end of the tests Laniki is exhausted. His muscles ache from tension and excitement. The fatigue feels good, though, because all his arrows hit the mark. He feels ten feet tall. He is now a true member of his people, united through the great Maraké.▲

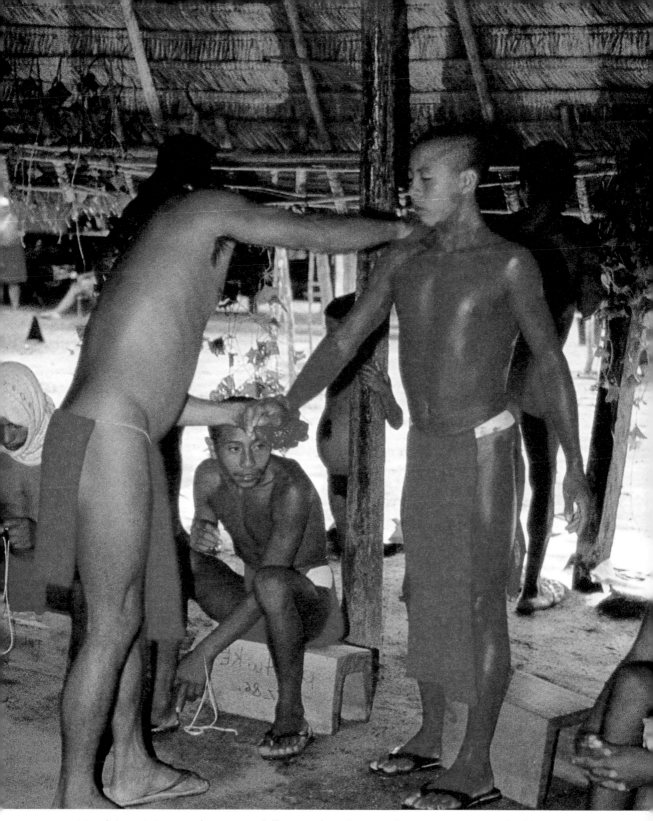

Maraké participants who successfully complete the test of temptation are marked by a reddish stain on their bodies.

CHAPTER 2

THE WAYANA

THE WAYANA ARE ONE OF THE MANY INDIGENOUS PEOPLES of South America. They are a rain forest people who live in the southern border regions of Suriname (formerly Dutch Guiana) and French Guiana along the upper Parú, Jarí, Marouini, Lawa, Palomeu, and Tapanahony rivers. They live in the Amazon jungle, a vast basin of 2,300,000 square miles fed by the waters of the Amazon River. Half of the Amazon forest is in Brazilian and Guianan territories. In the jungle the average temperature is 80°F. Rainfall measures from 160 to 400 inches a year.

Origins

Through physiological studies of Amerindians, the first inhabitants of the Americas, experts have traced their origin to Asia. They did not leave their land to conquer other peoples, but simply to hunt for game. In successive waves, entire peoples abandoned their Asiatic mountains and Mongolian plains to venture onto the strip of land that linked Asia and the Americas. In fact the Tiriós Indians have a story about their ancestors

The Wayana live in the hot and humid Amazon rain forest along small branches of the great Amazon River.

having crossed a land so cold that they had to dress in animal skins. The Tiriós live in the northeast Amazon, where the weather is never cold. The tale seems to be the communal recollection of crossing the Bering Strait through Alaska 50,000 years ago.

Originally, many of the Wayana lived in northern Brazil. After losing a battle against the ferocious Wayampi people, many of them fled across the Tumuc-Humac Mountains into what would later become Suriname and French Guiana. They live mostly along small rivers and are considered accomplished boatmen and fishermen.

Skill at fishing has enabled the Wayana to survive for centuries; even children participate.

It is estimated that before the arrival of the Europeans the population of what is now Suriname and French Guiana was 15,000 to 20,000. Since that time there has been a huge decline, principally because of the diseases that were introduced by the Europeans. Currently fewer than 1,000 indigenous people—Wayana, Wayampi, and Emerillon people—remain in the interior. Of that number, about 500 are Wayana. The Wayana are spread out among eight villages. Three quarters of them live on the Litani River in French Guiana; the remainder live along Suriname rivers.

The language of the Wayana is Cariban. It is a language spoken by several groups, but in each village it has its own unique dialect. Traditionally, the Wayana preserve their history orally, the elders of the village passing it from generation to generation in the form of stories and legends.

The Wayana are considered to be a people of the interior, meaning that their villages are not on the coastal shores of French Guiana, but deep inside the Amazon jungle. The three principal peoples of the interior, the Wayana, Oyampi, and Emerillon, are quite different linguistically and culturally, yet they are quite similar physiologically. Remarkably, they all have the same blood type, 0 positive.

Physical Characteristics

The Wayana have had sustained contact with the outside world for less than 20 years. Even though they trade on a limited scale with the industrialized world, they have preserved a rich cultural heritage. They are still very much a part of the forest ecosystem, depending on the environment for the majority of their material needs.

Wayana men wear a traditional red loincloth; the women wear a small cloth apron. They paint their bodies with *roucou*, a red dye obtained from the nut of a jungle plant. Both men and woman wear their hair long and pluck their eyelashes and eyebrows. They take great pride in their appearance.

The Wayana cherish pearls, which they obtain in trade. Some have trunks filled with the precious beads that they have acquired over the years. They adorn themselves in pearls for all festive occasions.

The Village

The Wayana have both patriarchal and matriarchal family settlements. Their households are organized around a common male or female ancestor. Formerly several families linked by a common ancestor lived in the same shelter, but the tendency today is toward more single-household dwellings. A chief supervises the settlement. The chief is either chosen by the villagers, or he inherits the position. He is advised by the mature married men of the village.

Family Shelters

Hut building among the Wayana is a male occupation. Permanent single-family shelters are grouped into small settlements. The most common structure is a rectangular hut with a pitched thatched roof. Most of these forest dwellings are one-room structures having no interior walls. There is little furniture, only hammocks for sleeping or daytime lounging, wooden benches carved into animal shapes, smoothed logs used for sitting, and fireplaces consisting of a few stones. The women store their domestic tools in baskets or hang them by string from the rafters.

The Wayana are considered seminomadic because they must rebuild their settlements several times during their lives. When the Wayana clear a patch of land and build their huts,

Constructing huts is the task of the men in a Wayana village. Because of insects and the damp climate, huts must be built often.

they destroy a natural balance. Slowly the Amazon forest begins to reclaim its land. Parasites and insects invade the wooden structures, and the wooden supports deteriorate and rot away. It is easier to rebuild than to try to repair the structures.

Farming
Hunting and fishing are the main means of survival for the Wayana, providing the necessary protein and fat in their diet. However, farming is actually most important, despite the obstacles presented by the hilly terrain and poor soil. The

19

The juice of the manioc root is used to make a traditional fermented beverage.

majority of Amerindians clear land for their farms along the shores of rivers that are navigable by canoe.

Each Wayana household has its own patch of land. They farm by the swidden, or slash-and-burn, method. First the men fell the trees and clear a one- to two-acre piece of land. Primitive axes of stone or iron are used. Large trees are left where they fall, and the smaller brush is piled up and burned. It is too difficult to transport the trees to a spot where they might be sold, so they are burned. The burning has one good side effect: It releases the nutrients of the trees into the soil. This gives a boost to the first few seasons of crops planted, but the effects are short-lived. Productivity decreases greatly after a few seasons, and the farmer must repeat the process on a new patch of land.

Manioc, which is planted from cuttings, is the basic crop. Before it can be used to make thin cakes or a fermented beverage, its natural poison must be removed. The Wayana also cultivate yams, sugarcane, bananas, and plantains. They plant and harvest only what is needed to nourish the household; very little is left that could be sold for profit. The Wayana supplement their farming by collecting nuts, insects, reptiles, honey, and wild fruits.

Fishing and Hunting

The Wayana are experienced and successful fishermen. They consume a large quantity of fish. They prefer spearfishing but are also known to use the hook-and-bait method. Sometimes

Rivers are vital resources to the Wayana. They use them for both practical and recreational purposes.

they fish by releasing the pulp from a poisonous vine into a small pool of water. The drug stuns the fish, and they float to the surface, where they are easily gathered.

The Wayana are also hunters, and many use rifles that they acquire through trade. The game includes deer, peccaries, tapirs, monkeys, armadillos, anteaters, sloths, and various birds. Before they had rifles, Wayana used spears, traps, arrows, and blowguns with poisoned darts.

Wayana villages and their farm plots are often widely separated along the river. Therefore transportation by canoe is vital. When the Wayana men are not hunting or fishing or tending their farms, they build or repair the dugout canoes.▲

CHAPTER 3

CUSTOMS AND BELIEFS

FORMAL RELIGION IS NOT PRACTICED BY THE WAYANA, BUT they do hold certain spiritual beliefs. They are animists, believing that everything has a spirit. The Wayana recognize a god or boss spirit but do not worship him. His existence is mentioned in myths, but he is not credited with the creation of the universe. The world as it is known to them is believed to have been created by a culture hero. A hero of this sort is found in many local myths throughout Suriname and French Guiana. Some of the names for him are Macunaima, Amalivaca, and Haburi. He is considered to be a child of the sun or some other heavenly body. In one myth, the hero does battle with a supernatural snake and kills it. From the snake's body emerge men, animals, and *binas* (hunting charms). In another myth the hero breaks off parts of a magical tree, each part then turning into a different type of animal.

The Wayana Shaman

In Wayana society, the shaman is both a healer and prophet. The Wayana believe that everyone has the potential to become

The Wayana are animists and believe that everything has a spirit. They attribute their existence to a hero, perhaps a child of the sun.

a shaman. Only those who see into and communicate with the spirit world succeed. A shaman may be familiar with and use more than 100 plant species for healing purposes. His power comes from this knowledge.

One senses an energy between the shaman and the forest. He is at home in both the physical and spirit worlds and is responsible for maintaining the equilibrium between the two. Even the weather is believed to be under his control. The Wayana believe that the survival of their village depends on how well the shaman communicates with the spirit world. He is also

The Moloko, or shaman, is the communicator between the spirits and the people. He performs the important task of curing illness within the community.

the keeper of the people's traditions and lore and offers guidance on proper spiritual conduct.

The Wayana shaman's most important role is that of healer. According to shaman tradition, illness results from the breaking of a taboo, the casting of a spell, the anger of the gods, or disharmony between the physical and spirit worlds. A shaman is able to treat many illnesses with traditional cures. Colds and coughs are treated with renealmía, which is a type of ginger. Some Wayana suffer from "electric eel disease." Its symptoms resemble those of epilepsy and of the effects of a shock by an electric eel. To treat this disease they boil the leaves of a wild pepper bush called a *ku-mah-ne-mah* in a closed pot; then they let the steam escape under the hammock of the sick person. For cases that resist treatment with plants alone, the shaman consults the spirit world to learn the origin of the disease and its cure.

To consult the spirit world, the shaman must enter a trance. This can be done by smoking or eating hallucinogenic substances, dancing, chanting, or beating rhythmically on a drum. The shaman may wear symbolic clothing or ritual objects such as rattles or mirrors. The smoking of tobacco is often part of the ritual because it is believed to have curative powers.

The Wayana believe that each person has a spirit within called *akawale*. During a healing trance, the shaman examines the spirit to see if it has any holes. Bad spirits are everywhere and are always trying to get into the *akawale*. If a hole is found, it indicates that the sick person has probably been bewitched.

A Wayana craftsman tests the sound of a flute he is making. Playing musical instruments is a favorite activity of the Wayana.

When weak spots or holes are found in the *akawale,* the shaman repairs them by sucking out the bad spirits.

A shaman also uses such therapies as relaxation, massage, and hypnosis, as well as changes in diet. Many of these therapies are being examined by Western doctors.

For many indigenous peoples, contact with the outside world has had a profoundly detrimental effect on traditional healing practices. For instance, the missionaries and their desire to bring Christianity to the Amerindians in this region contributed to the downfall of shamanism. About 20 years ago the missionaries came to the Tiriós people in Suriname.

Their people were very sick with a disease that had been introduced by Europeans, and the shaman was not able to cure them. Western medicine worked well against the new diseases. The Tiriós accepted both the missionaries' god and their medicine. The shamans lost their power.

Missionaries were forbidden by the national government to practice in French Guiana. Consequently, Wayana living in Suriname crossed the Marouini River into French Guiana to avoid conflict with the missionaries. Thus the Wayana shamans were able to continue to live by the old ways. Today shamanism thrives in the Wayana villages.

A shaman does not live forever, so it is important that his knowledge and skills be handed down to younger generations. Although the Wayana believe that everyone has the potential to become a shaman, they traditionally prefer for their sons to be apprentices.

Recreation

The most popular form of social amusement is dancing and singing to music. Dance movements imitate animals or birds. Musical instruments played are the flute, drum, and fiddle.

At home in the evenings the Wayana tell stories and sometimes act them out. They are also fond of practical jokes.

The children spend their days following the adults around. They play games of hunting and fishing, using miniature spears and clubs. Using domestic tools, they pretend to cook or weave. They also love to play and dive in the river rapids.

Wayana infants are believed to have a special connection with their fathers. After the observance of a ritual called the *couvade,* during which the father may not leave the village, children are named. Names are kept secret, however.

Puberty

The great Maraké is the most important puberty ritual, although people of all ages participate. The adolescent boys are subjected to stinging insects that are held in frames against their skin. Other proofs of passage into adulthood are work ordeals such as the clearing of a field, the building of a house, or hunting.

Wayana girls are secluded in the bush or in a special structure during their first menstruation. They are required to abstain from certain foods during this time.

Marriage

Young people choose their own spouse. Formerly the Wayana were endogamous, meaning they were limited to marriage within their village. This practice was an attempt to keep the village intact. Currently the Wayana are exogamous and freely marry outside their own village.

Once a man has chosen a bride, he must earn the right to marry her through some sort of service to the prospective father-in-law. Once they are married, the groom will live with his wife under the roof of his new father-in-law and abide by his word. The couple is permitted to leave the home when the in-laws have died. Usually they move to the home of the husband. Polygamy, the practice of having two or more wives, is permitted but is not widely observed.

When there are more unmarried men than unmarried women in a village, Wayana men leave their village to attend a courting festival in another settlement. They wear their finest headdresses and beaded necklaces to make the best possible impression.

Wayana women spend much of their time weaving, preparing food, and taking care of children. For celebrations, they prepare the ceremonial garments and headdresses. Often older daughters watch over younger siblings so that the mother can tend to these tasks. The work is difficult and time-consuming.

Childbirth

In the past, when a woman knew that the time was drawing near for her child to be born, she went out into the bush to give birth. Today the women usually give birth in their huts. Certain rituals still surround the event. It is believed that a special connection exists between the spirit of the child and its father. Once the infant is born, the father must remain in the village for a specified time called the *couvade*. It is believed that harm will come to the child if the father goes into the bush during that period.

At the end of the *couvade* the infant receives his name from the shaman. The name, which is secret, usually refers to some aspect of the child's appearance or to his resemblance to an animal or plant. In Wayana society it is not permitted to call people by name in direct conversation. Many people adopt public names for everyday use. Speaking the names of the deceased is also taboo.

When Wayana girls reach puberty and experience their first menstruation, they must be secluded and avoid eating certain foods.

Mourning

When a family member dies, Wayana relatives cut their hair and discontinue wearing ornaments for a certain period of time. The hut of the deceased is abandoned. The corpse is cremated, and the ashes are kept by a window. The entire village joins in the final mourning ceremony, a dance that is believed to drive away evil spirits.

The Wayana remain firmly attached to their beliefs and customs. They celebrate their rituals with astounding vigor. It is through these customs and beliefs that their villages have survived and live in harmony. ▲

Crafts are an important means for the Wayana to maintain cultural traditions.

Colonizers were interested in economic gain when they came to the Americas and had little concern for the people they encountered.

CHAPTER 4

COLONIZATION

THE GUIANAS WERE DISCOVERED DURING THE EXPEDITION of Amerigo Vespucci in 1499. This region was explored the following year by Vincent Pinzon and again in 1596 by Sir Walter Raleigh. The Guianas were particularly interesting to the colonial powers because they were believed to have huge resources of gold.

In the early 1500s the colonial powers were busy carving up the Americas for themselves. Spain was actively pursuing interests in western South America. The Dutch, English, and Portuguese were establishing colonial territories in the Amazon region.

The French tried a few times to settle the Cayenne peninsula during the 1600s, but were unsuccessful. French merchant companies were unable to prosper. Territorial disputes arose between France and The Netherlands, but in 1776 an expedition succeeded in securing a portion of Guiana for France.

It appears that the French made no attempt to enslave the Wayana or seize their land. Contact with the colonists was for the most part confined to trade.

French Guiana became an overseas department by law in 1946. All residents of French Guiana obtained the same rights as the citizens of France. In 1950 the trading post at Maripasoula was founded. At that point the Wayana came in direct contact with the Europeans, and their material life changed drastically. They were able to trade for modern tools and rifles. Some Wayana even obtained small outboard motors for their canoes.

Despite their limited contact with the Europeans, however, the population of the Wayana declined significantly. They were extremely susceptible to the diseases of the Europeans. Recently the French Guiana government has begun building infirmaries in some of the villages, where the Wayana can be examined and treated by doctors.▲

In Wayana village schools, students study the Wayana language as well as subjects like geography and math. The Wayana resisted pressure to educate their children in French.

It is the hope of the Wayana that those who are able to read will learn even more about their own rich culture and heritage. They would like to see the Wayana legends and tales written out for future generations.

The Amerindian Association of French Guiana

Recently there has been a political awakening of the Amerindians, who for so long submitted to external influences and accepted change imposed by the French Guiana government.

Under the supervision of several young Galibi Indians, six indigenous peoples of French Guiana decided to form the

Traditional celebrations, such as this dance following rites of initiation, provide a source of cultural pride at a time when the Wayana are under a barrage of Western influences.

Amerindian Association of French Guiana (AAGF)—Emerillon, Palikour, Wayana, Wayampi, Arawak, and Galibi. Félix Tiouka, Paul Henri, and Guillaume Apollinaire were the first indigenous people to dare to approach the political powers of French Guiana. The goal of the AAGF is to attain recognition of the rights of Amerindians and to promote their culture.

The AAGF has met with a great success. The government repealed a collective property tax that was imposed on each people, which is a large step toward the recognition of the peoples' ownership of their collective property. The AAGF is also working toward regulations prohibiting the sale of indigenous lands.

The Western world and its constant pressures are no more than a few hours away from Wayana territory by canoe. The effects are visible in the dress of the young people, who have begun to abandon pearls and body painting for T-shirts and shorts. Wayana men earn money by acting as guides for European expeditions. Wayana leaders believe that for their culture to survive everyone must work together to safeguard the rights of Amerindian peoples. They have confidence in their children and hope that they will be able to face their future with courage and strength.▲

The Wayana have used medicinal plants from the rain forest to keep themselves healthy for hundreds of years. As these children grow up, they may find that much of the rain forest has been carelessly exploited for its wood and other resources.

The Rain Forest

Rain forest plants are providing Western scientists with tens of thousands of new compounds that show potential as antiviral agents. Shaman Pharmaceuticals of northern California focuses its research on plants used medicinally by rain forest peoples. It has already developed compounds that seem to be effective against two viruses in human clinical trials.

The National Cancer Institute has increased its efforts to find and test new rain forest plant compounds against the AIDS virus and various cancers.

The indigenous peoples of the Amazon rain forest are important to this effort. The indigenous peoples have maintained their own identity as well as their own ethnopharmacopoeia (knowledge and use of local medicinal plants). There are Western ethnobotanists in the rain forest today gathering plant samples and spending time with shamans to learn their secrets.

The peoples themselves do destroy natural resources, as in the case of their slash-and-burn method of farming. However, they are devoted conservationists. For example, when they need sap from a tree to use as glue for the construction of canoes, they do not chop down the tree. They merely score the bark and collect the sap as it runs out. This method can be repeated often without damage to the tree.

Unfortunately, rain forests and their people the world over are endangered. The rain forests are being destroyed for their timber, iron, and gold and to obtain more agricultural land for the ever increasing population. One third of the Amazon rain forest has already disappeared. If the destruction continues at its present rate, nearly one fifth of the world's remaining rain forest territory will be destroyed by the year 2000.

Scientists are studying the rain forest because they believe that it may hold the key to curing many diseases. The Wayana value the rain forest and use its resources wisely.

NEIGHBORING PEOPLES

THE TIRIÓS ARE ONE OF THE CLOSEST NEIGHBORING peoples of the Wayana. They live along the Sipaliwini River in southwest Suriname and the Boven Tapanahony River in the southeast. The Wayana and the **Tiriós** live together in the village of Tepoe east of the Lawa River. The Tiriós are expert hunters and gatherers. They speak Cariban with their own dialect, but it does not prevent them from communicating with the Wayana.

The **Oyampi** are linguistically and culturally different from the Wayana but quite similar physiologically. The Oyampi speak Tupi-Guarani. The population is small: About 300 Oyampi live along the Oyapok and Kouk Rivers. The Oyampi are a very closed people. They rarely visit neighboring villages, and very few marriages occur outside the village.

Their villages are stable. Unlike the Wayana, they do not move. This may have to do with their customs. They bury their dead in a cemetery, and they gather regularly at the tombs of deceased family members.

During the colonial period the Portuguese tried to enslave the Amerindians. This attempt met with disastrous results. The Amerindians sickened and died when taken from their villages and forced into slave labor. Consequently the Portuguese brought cargoes of slaves from Africa, the first Africans in Brazil.

In the 18th century a large number of these slaves escaped into the jungles of Suriname south of the Marouini River. There they formed new peoples called the **Boni**. The Boni assembled their villages along the Lawa River in the Marouini Basin and became great navigators. They have villages in both Suriname and French Guiana but enjoy a wide independence from the two governments. They too have stable villages, and their population has grown more steadily than those of the Amerindians.

The Wayana and Boni live in the same region peacefully, but their relationship is limited to trade.

The Boni are unique because they have adopted the best parts of the European culture, yet remain faithful to their African roots. Their language is Taki-Tak, which is derived from English. They are builders and specialize in transportation. They have developed their own interesting and elaborate form of art. The doors and walls of their huts are adorned with detailed paintings and carvings. The huts reveal the European influence in their complicated and permanent construction.▲

FACTS ABOUT THE WAYANA

Population: Approximately 500

Location: Suriname and French Guiana, South America

Environment: Amazon jungle and rain forest

Rainfall: 160-400 inches per year

Climate: Hot and humid

Language: Cariban

Main Activities: Fishing, hunting, farming

Animals: Deer, peccary, tapir, monkeys, armadillo, anteater

Religion: Animism

GLOSSARY

akawale The spirit of a human being.

animism Belief that every animate and inanimate thing has a soul.

Boni A people in Suriname and French Guiana descended from African slaves.

couvade Ritual period after the birth of a child.

epa Board used almost like a drum stamped upon in the Maraké ceremony.

ku-mah-ne-mah Wild pepper bush with healing qualities.

kunana Insect-filled frame used in the Maraké tests.

liana Climbing vine, especially of tropical rain forests.

olok Ceremonial feathered headdress.

Oyampi An Amerindian people.

Tiriós An Amerindian people.

toukousipan Ceremonial house.

FOR FURTHER READING

Bernard, Patrick. *Les Oubliés du Temps.* Xonrupt-Longemer: Anako Editions, 1991.

Caufield, Catherine. *In The Rainforest.* New York: Knopf, 1985.

French Embassy Press Information Service. *French Guiana, A Geographical and Historical Survey.* Washington, D.C., 1994.

Hames, R. and Vickers, W. *Adaptive Responses of Native Amazonians.* New York: Academic Press, 1983.

Hurault, Jean. *Africains de Guyane.* The Hague: Mouton, 1970.

Plotkin, Mark J. *Tales of a Shaman's Apprentice.* New York: Viking, 1993.

———. "An Earthly Paradise Regained." *Americas,* Jan./Feb. 1994.

Plotkin, Mark J., and Famolare, Lisa. *Sustainable Harvest and Marketing of Rain Forest Products.* Washington, D.C.: Island Press, 1992.

Steward, Julian. *Handbook of South American Indians.* Washington, D.C.: Smithsonian Institution, 1946-1959.

Steward, Julian, and Faron, Louis C. *Native Peoples of South America.* New York: McGraw-Hill, 1959.

INDEX

Photo Credits: ©Anako Editions/Patrick Bernard, André Cognat
Layout and Design: Kim Sonsky

Master Index

INDIGENOUS PEOPLES OF THE WORLD

Master Index

INDIGENOUS PEOPLES OF THE WORLD

This index is a compilation of the indices of all 12 volumes in this set. Volume numbers appear in **bold** type; the page numbers within that volume follow in plain type. For example, angels, **6:**31, 33 indicates that angels are referred to in volume 6 (*Maya*) on pages 31 and 33.

DATE DUE

1001			
753			
1004			

HIGHSMITH   #45102